D0754694

Bawdy Songs
of the Early Music Hall

Selected, with an introduction, by
George Speaight

David & Charles
Newton Abbot/London/Vancouver

ISBN 0 7153 7013 8

Printed in Great Britain
by Redwood Burn Ltd, Trowbridge & Esher
for David & Charles (Holdings) Limited
South Devon House Newton Abbot Devon
Published in Canada
by Douglas David & Charles Limited
132 Philip Avenue North Vancouver BC

Contents

Illustrations

Acknowledgements

The publisher wishes to express his appreciation of the facilities granted by the British Library at the British Museum for the photography of the song books and music sheets reproduced here; and to John Freeman for taking the photographs.

Introduction

The English music hall had its origins in the 'song and supper
rooms' that came into popularity in the early decades of the
nineteenth century. There had, of course, always been a
tradition of tavern sing-songs but by the 1830s a number of
establishments in London had gained a reputation for providing
food and drink, accompanied by regular singing. The songs
were, in the beginning, sung by the landlord or the patrons
of the house, but gradually semi-professional and then fully
professional singers were introduced to build up a programme.
The proprietor of the house acted as chairman of the proceed-
ings. The patrons joined lustily in the choruses. And a convivial evening was enjoyed by all.

The clientele for these establishments was exclusively male
and was largely drawn from the ranks of the wilder journalists,
lawyers, soldiers and young Corinthians. There are a handful
of references in the literature and memoirs of the period to
enable us to recapture something of the atmosphere of these
assemblies, but they were never described in detail and
were, indeed, regarded as far from respectable. We must
build up their picture from hints and veiled allusions.

During the Regency and early Victorian period two houses
of this kind enjoyed particular popularity: these were the
Cider Cellars in Maiden Lane and the Coal Hole in Fountain
Court, off the Strand. Pierce Egan describes how some
Regency bucks found their pleasure 'in diving night after
night into the **Cellar** to hear a good **chaunt**: although emitting
volumes of smoke like a furnace, and crowded together like
the Black Hole in Calcutta' [1] During the 1820s and early 1830s
these houses came under the management of the brothers
William and John Rhodes, who conducted them as resorts for
the midnight revelries of a gay band of bohemian men-about-
town. Similar to these was Offley's in King Street, Covent
Garden, where the Wednesday sing-songs, conducted
mostly by gifted amateurs, attracted a packed house of
'baby bucks, black-legs and half-pay officers'.[2] Recalling these
establishments many years later, George Sims wrote: 'The
Coal Hole and the Cider Cellars are names of imperishable
memory, because they are landmarks in the story of the night
life of London when night was apparently given up to drinking
and rowdyism, and a rollicking and full-flavoured conviviality
that the present generation would consider outrageous.'[3]

Perhaps the best description of the 'singing houses which
these roaring young blades frequented' is provided by
Thackeray, who was certainly writing from personal exper-

ience. In **Pendennis**, set in the mid 1830s, he describes the Back Kitchen of the Fielding's Head in the Covent Garden area, where the clientele attracted by the jolly singing and suppers included country tradesmen and farmers in London for business, squads of young apprentices and assistants, rakish young medical students, young university bucks, handsome young guardsmen, florid bucks from the St James's Street Clubs, young barristers like Pen and his friend, and even members of the House of Peers. Dishes like sausages and mash, Welsh rabbit, poached eggs and kidneys, or devilled turkey were served, and the drink might be stout, punch, brandy, whisky, sherry and water, gin twist, or even champagne cup.

The landlord of the Back Kitchen, who was noted for his jolly appearance and fine voice, generally took the chair that was reserved for 'the president of the night's entertainment ... He used to sing profusely in the course of the harmonic meeting, and his songs were of what may be called the British Brandy and Water School of Song—such as ''The Good old English Gentleman'', ''Dear Tom, this Brown Jug'', and so forth—songs in which pathos and hospitality are blended, and the praises of good liquor and the social affections are chanted in a baritone voice. The charms of our women, the heroic deeds of our naval and military commanders, are often sung in the ballads of this school.' The music to accompany the singers or in the intervals of the songs was provided by a battered piano, played upon by a musician lately from the orchestra of a provincial theatre. The singers tended to sit at a special singers' table; some of them were regular patrons of the house, like Captain Costigan, others might be noted vocalists who made the rounds of these rooms and places like Vauxhall Gardens; such a one was the bass, described by Thackeray, who gave an impressive rendering of a song called 'The Body Snatcher', for which he was revealed on the drawing of a curtain 'in the character of the Snatcher, sitting on a coffin, with a flask of gin before him, with a spade, and a candle stuck in a skull. The song was sung with a really admirable terrific humour. The singer's voice went down so low, that its grumbles rumbled into the hearer's awe-stricken soul; and in the chorus he clamped with his spade and gave a demoniac ''Ha! ha!'' which caused the very glasses to quiver on the table, as with terror.'[4]

Not all the songs sung at these houses, however, were such dramatic fare, still less were they in praise of 'the charms of our women'. As night wore on, songs of another description might be heard. Recalling these establishments in the 1870s, Blanchard Jerrold wrote: 'How long ago is it since gentlemen of the highest degree went to the Cider Cellars and the Coal Hole? Speculating on the changes in London at play, within the last five-and-twenty years, in that corner of Evans's where, any night, you could tell at once by a sudden influx that the House was up; we trundle back through the seasons, to the time when the bar parlour of the Cider Cellars—a dirty, stifling, underground tavern in Maiden Lane, behind the Strand—was the meeting place from Fop's Alley, after the opera. The Cave of Harmony was a cellar for shameful song-singing—where members of both Houses, the pick of the Universities, and the bucks of the Row, were content to dwell in indecencies for ever. When there was a burst of unwonted enthusiasm, you might be certain that some genius of the place had soared to a happy combination of indecency with blasphemy.'[5]

It was of the Cave of Harmony at Evans's in King Street, Covent Garden, that Thackeray wrote, 'there was once a time . . . when the acme of pleasure seemed to be . . . to dine at the Piazza, go to the play and see Braham in **Fra Diavolo**, and end the frolic evening by partaking of supper and a song at the "Cave of Harmony"'.[6] Here Colonel Newcome brought his young son in the expectation of enjoying an evening of glee singing and old English ballads, but when later in the evening Captain Costigan rose to his feet and gave voice to a song, it so offended the worthy Colonel that he called for silence. When some in the room urged the singer to go on, the Colonel retorted, 'Does any gentleman say "Go on"? Does any man who has a wife and sisters, or children at home, say "Go on" to such disgusting ribaldry as this? Do you dare, sir, to call yourself a gentleman, and to say that you hold the king's commission, and to sit down amongst Christians and men of honour, and defile the ears of young boys with this wicked balderdash?' 'Why do you bring young boys here, old boy?' cried one of the diners, as the Colonel stalked, with his son, from the room.

The Songs

What were these songs that were so unsuitable for a boy's ears, that so offended Colonel Newcome, that produced a burst of unwonted enthusiasm in the smoke-filled cellars of the Cave of Harmony or the Cole Hole?

The texts of the songs that Regency swells and Victorian bucks sang in their cups seemed to have vanished in a bonfire of mid-Victorian disapproval. A fortunate discovery, however, made at the British Museum during my research into the history of the English toy theatre, to which I was led by a clue provided by Mr Gerald Morice, has revealed a cache of slim booklets published by the theatrical printseller, William West, at 57 Wych Street, Strand. They carry such titles as **The Randy Songster** or **The Cuckold's Nest of Choice, Flash, Smutty and Delicious Songs** and record the songs sung at the Coal Hole, the Cider Cellars, Offley's and, no doubt, similar establishments. As far as I am aware, they have never been reprinted, and, indeed, their existence was practically unknown and unrecorded, apart from an entry in Ashbee's bibliography of pornographic books[7] and an inaccurate reference in Ivan Bloch's **Sexual Life in England** of 1901.

In the present permissive atmosphere it seems justifiable to republish a selection of these songs, and thus enable twentieth-century readers to study this aspect of early nineteenth-century social life, to estimate their place in the development of the music hall, and—why should we deny it? —to enjoy, I hope, these examples of Regency and early Victorian bawdiness.

The Bawdy Tradition

Bawdy songs have a long and a not dishonourable place in the English tradition. Shakespeare knew them, and when Ophelia lost her wits her mind ran upon a vulgar country ditty that the author must have learnt in the Warwickshire lanes :

> . . . Alack, and fie for shame
> Young men will do't, if they come to't,
> By cock they are to blame . . .

When Cecil Sharp was collecting folk songs at the end of the nineteenth century, he carefully recorded (though he failed at that time to print) uninhibited folk songs like 'Gently Johnny my Jingaloo'

> . . . I put my hand all on her knee
> She says to me do you want to see?
>   I put my hand all on her thigh
> She says to me do you want to try?
>   I put my hand all on her billy
> She says to me do you want to fell 'ee?
>   I put my hand all on her head
> She says you want my maidenhead.

When Tom D'Urfey compiled his famous collection of songs under the familiar title of **Pills to purge Melancholy** in 1719, he included many a bawdy ballad set to familiar airs:

> My pretty maid, I fain would know
> What thing it is will breed delight,
> That thrives to stand, yet cannot go,
> That feeds the mouth that cannot bite . . .
>
> It is a shaft of Cupid's cut,
> 'Twill serve to rove, to prick, to butt.
> There's never a maid but, by her will,
> Will keep it in her quiver still.

Henry Purcell did not think it beneath his dignity to set an air to the following catch:

> My Lady's coachman John being married to her maid,
> Her Ladyship did hear on't and to him thus she said,
> 'I never had a wench so handsome in my life
> I prithee therefore tell me how you got such a wife.'
> John star'd her in the face and answer'd very blunt,
> 'E'en as my Lord got you.' 'How's that?' 'Why by the
>   cunt.'

Robert Burns collected, edited, and in some cases contributed to the lively collection of Scottish ribald verses that appeared as **The Merry Muses of Caledonia** in about 1800.

The songs in this collection are clearly in a tradition that goes back, through the lighter moments of Burns, Purcell, D'Urfey and Shakespeare to Chaucer and the Middle Ages, and that goes forward behind the veil of Victorian respectability to the songs we sang on route marches in the Army or that rugby players sing in their baths today. They are unashamedly vulgar and licentious, but they surely reflect a fundamentally healthy approach to life. Men are made for maids, who shall not long remain so; sex is fun – for women as much as for men; life is full of glorious and unexpected encounters; let us enjoy them while we can. Of course, real life is not like this; the whole thing is a fantasy; after nine months comes the reckoning; but for the moment we sing and make merry.

All the songs at these 'free and easies' were intended to be sung to music that was already familiar. Some of them were new words set to the tunes of earlier bawdy songs of the eighteenth century; see, for example, 'There's Somebody Coming' and 'The Maid and the Fishmonger', which fit the tunes of bawdy songs of the 1770s. But most of them are described as to be sung to the air of some popular ballad of the period, and where I have been able to trace these I have reproduced the music and some verses at least of these originals. These will not only enable owners of this book to sing some of the songs themselves, if they wish, but they illustrate another facet of popular bawdy song making – that of parody. The contrast between the musical score intended for a drawing room ballad and the vulgarity of the new words is sometimes very droll, and no little wit is displayed in some of the substitutions of words, so that, to quote just a couple of examples from this collection,

> Oh there's no love like the first love
> For constancy and truth

becomes

> There is no shove like the first shove
> For ecstasy and bliss;

or

> I love, oh how I love to ride
> On the fierce, foaming, bursting tide

becomes

> I love, oh how I love to ride
> My hot, my wheedling, coaxing bride.

Parody was an art at which the early Victorians excelled, and some of these 'famous amatory parodies' are not unworthy examples of the **genre.**

The Publisher

The publisher of these booklets is a surprising figure to be discovered on the fringe of the pornographic book trade. William West was a printseller who, in 1811, conceived the idea of printing sheets of small characters and scenery for the popular plays of the day. These developed into a flourishing toy theatre industry, which attracted some hundred publishers and printsellers during the next fifty or sixty years. West was the first and probably the best of the publishers of the Juvenile Drama, as it was called. [8]

West's first place of business was in Exeter Street; he moved to Wych Street, opposite the Olympic Theatre, in 1823; his last new toy theatre play was published in 1831 but he continued to reprint from the old plates and to sell old stock up to his death in 1854. There are curious accounts of him in his last years, dressed in shabby old clothes, fondling a tame fox, and wheezing in his last illness behind the thin partition between the shop and his bedroom. In 1850 he was interviewed by Henry Mayhew, who recorded a fascinating account of his reminiscences as the original toy theatre publisher. [9]

West made no reference to his bawdy song books in his interview with Mayhew, but from internal evidence it would appear that he embarked upon the publication of these booklets in the mid-1830s, probably after he ceased issuing new toy theatres plays. I am afraid he may have found them more profitable! A song (not included in this collection) entitled 'The Irish Policeman' must be subsequent to the establishment of the London Metropolitan Police Force in 1829; another song entitled 'Riding Saint George' refers to Andrew Ducrow's performance in **Saint George and the Dragon**, which was produced at Covent Garden in 1833; among various 'unbawdy' songs which are included to fill the volumes out is Thomas Rice's famous song 'Jim Crow', which was first sung in London in 1836; and one called 'The Bill Sticker' refers to Charles Matthews's association with Madame Vestris, which began at the Olympic in 1835 and led to their marriage in 1838.

The coarseness of these songs may offend us today – and there are some featuring scatalogical humour and an obsession with venereal disease that I have not cared to reprint – but we should see them in the atmosphere of the times as representing another facet of the lusty theatrical life of the period. Many a grave mid-Victorian gentleman must have bellowed these choruses out in the days of his youth. As the music hall developed by the middle of the century into a place of public entertainment, with the singing much more important than the drinking, songs as outspoken as these had to be banished. The songs that took their place, with their reflection of working class life and ambitions, are of greater value to the sociological student. But it was bawdy songs such as these that helped to create the robust singing tradition that was to give the music hall its superb character.

It is, too, a droll thought that while children were examining toy theatre sheets on the counter of the Wych Street shop, these coarse and vulgar booklets were lying under the counter! But the toy theatre and the Coal Hole were really not all that far apart. Wych Street was not only the site of the Olympic Theatre but – with the adjoining Holywell Street – was notorious for its pornographic bookshops. West catered for both aspects of Regency taste. Henry Spencer Ashbee, who may even have been one of his customers as a boy (he was born in 1834), made an elaborate apology for him while listing his 'jovial, smutty ditties' and describes him as 'a man of artistic feeling and good repute'. [10]

The authorship of these songs was, as might be expected, anonymous. The statement by Ivan Bloch that they were written by West himself is almost certainly inaccurate. A few of the songs are credited to J. W. A. and J. H. L., whoever they may be, and a few more are described 'as written and sung by Mr J. H. Munyard'. J. H. Munyard was a minor actor who specialised in comic songs: in 1833, aged only sixteen, he had joined the company at the little Westminster Theatre, Tothill Street; he appeared in several provincial theatres, notably at the Theatre Royal, Norwich, where he published a slim collection of songs for his Benefit in 1840; in 1844 he was at Brighton, where he was sufficiently popular with the military to persuade the Colonel and officers of the 6th Inniskillens to patronise his Benefit; the same year he joined the Adelphi company under Madame Celeste, where he made a mark for himself as 'a very excellent second low comedian'. [11] He died in 1850 at the early age of thirty-five. The shadowy portrait of one, at least, of the author-singers of these bawdy songs begins to emerge from the world of the minor theatres and the provincial circuits.

A singer called Joe Wells is recalled as having often appeared at the Coal Hole, 'a dreadful old creature . . . who used to sing most disgusting ditties', [12] although they were 'somewhat relieved by a broad and racy humour'. One suspects his hand in the present collection. For the rest we know the names of some other singers: Tom Hudson, a favourite at the Cider Cellars, who is said to have parodied the melodies of Thomas Moore with rare ability; Jack Sharp, a comic vocalist at the Mogul in Drury Lane and the Doctor Johnson in Bolt Court as well as at Evans's; Charles Sloman, a noted **improvisatore**, who could invent rhymes on the spur of the moment about any person who happened to be in the room; W. G. Ross, famous for his rendering of 'Sam Hall'; and some others, many of them associated with the theatres of the day. To what extent the bawdy songs were a speciality of only a few singers, or whether most, or all, the vocalists sang them is not clear; nor do we know the proportion of bawdy to comic, sentimental or patriotic songs in a typical night's repertoire. Some accounts merely hint that 'there were one or two points in the song [at the Cider Cellars] at which very staid people might have taken a slight exception', [13] but there seems to be general agreement that the entertainment at these places 'consisted of songs of the erotic and bacchanalian order'. [14] The proprietors of the Canterbury Theatre of Varieties, the leader in a new school of family music halls, were emphatic, in a description of their theatre written in 1876, in describing how the entertainment there, in the early 1850s, had provided 'a perfect contrast to the other halls', such as the Coal Hole and the Cyder Cellars, where vulgar and indecent songs were then the order of the day'.

Over thirty titles are known to have been published by West in this series. They are all 48 page, 32-mo volumes, and this edition reproduces the original typography – with the occasional misprints; each volume is provided with a charming, slightly lubricious but in no way pornographic hand-coloured folding frontispiece, several examples of which are reproduced here. The volumes from which the songs reprinted in this collection have been selected are the following:

The Ri-Tum Ti-Tum Songster
The Frisky Vocalist
The Comic Songster and Gentleman's Private Cabinet
The Luscious Songster
The Icky-Wicky Songster
The New Cockalorum Songster
The Bang-Up Songster
The Cuckold's Nest
The Cockchafer
Nancy Dawson's Cabinet of Choice Songs

Similar volumes, referring also to the Coal Hole or the Cider Cellar, were published by 'H. Smith' (a pseudonym of the notorious pornographer, W. Dugdale) of 37 Holywell Street, and by John Duncombe, a perfectly respectable publisher, of Holborn Hill. [15] One could certainly fill many volumes with an extensive collection of these bawdy songs of the early music hall. But there is, to tell the truth, little variety as they chronicle with obsessive emphasis the exploits of 'Cupid's battering ram' as it seeks 'the beauties of the c---'.

Notes

1 Pierce Egan, **Life in London, or Tom and Jerry**, 1821, chapter 2.

2 'Bernard Blackmantle' (C. M. Westmacott), **The English Spy**, 1825, chapter headed 'Metropolitan Sketches'.

3 George R. Sims, **My Life: 60 Years of Bohemian London**, 1916.

4 William Thackeray, **The History of Pendennis**, 1848, chapters 30 and **inter alia** 19, 36, 39, 46, 55.

5 Gustave Doré, **London: a Pilgrimage**, 1872.

6 William Thackeray, **The Newcomes,** 1855, chapter 1.

7 "Pisanus Fraxi" (Henry Spencer Ashbee), **Index Librorum Prohibitorum**, 1877.

8 George Speaight, **The History of the English Toy Theatre**, 1969.

9 Reprinted in **Theatre Notebook** vol. xxvi no. 3, 1972, and, slightly abbreviated, in E. P. Thompson and Eileen Yeo, **The Unknown Mayhew**, 1971.

10 See note 7.

11 Edmund Yates, **Recollections and Experiences**, 1884, vol. i chapter 5. Also playbills at the Enthoven Collection, Victoria and Albert Museum, and the British Museum.

12 Edmund Yates, **op cit.**, vol. i chapter 4.

13 Albert Smith, **The Adventures of Mr. Ledbury**, 1847, vol. i chapter 18.

14 Charles Douglas Stuart and A. J. Park, **The Variety Stage: a History of the Music Halls from the Earliest Period to the Present Time**, 1895, chapter 2. Later works with useful chapters on the Song and Supper Rooms are Harold Scott, **The Early Doors**, 1946; M. Willson Disher, **Winkles and Champagne**, 1938; and D. F. Cheshire, **Music Hall in Britain**, 1974.

15 See note 7.

Notes to the Songs

Most of the sexual slang used in these songs is still in current use, though the basic four-letter Anglo-Saxon monosyllables are never employed. A few terms may, however, be unfamiliar to modern readers:

page 23 'The Maid and the Fishmonger', The word 'ling' as well as its normal meaning for a kind of sea fish, had a nineteenth-century slang meaning as the female sexual organ, as in the term 'ling-grappling'. It appears from this song that it was also applied to the female sexual odour. This definition is not recorded in Partridge's **Dictionary of Slang and Unconventional English** but he gives a twentieth-century Australian usage of the word as 'a stink'. It seems possible that there is an association of ideas here, and it is interesting to observe this hitherto unrecorded English usage of the 1830s to be current in Australia a century later. Perhaps it was carried there by transported convicts.

pages 50 and 66 'The Bower that Stands in Thigh Lane' and 'The Wonderful Belly Physic'. The word 'spend' was the usual Victorian term for the male sexual emission.

page 42 'O What a Queer Sensation'. The air for this song, described as 'Merrily Danced the Quaker's Wife', is the same as that chosen by Robert Burns for his song 'Blythe have I been on yon Hill', printed in 1799.

From win-dows las---ses look'd, a score,

Neighbours met at ev'--ry door, Sol-dier lads charm'd ev'--ry sight, For

eyes beam'd pleasure hearts danc'd light. Twas in the merry month of May, When bees from

flower to flower did hum, Soldiers thro' the town march'd gay, And all resolv'd to follow the drum

A capital Flash Song, now first printed.

Air—*Follow the Drum.*

Twas in the merry month of May,
When lasses feel so very queer,
Soldiers through the town did stray,
    And among the rest a drummer fair.
The ladies flock'd, a lively set,
Among the rest was jovial Bet,
Who well knew how to do 'he trick,
And all they wanted was the drummer's
    stick.

Twas, &c.

Roger's wife cried to a lad,
    Who beat the drum with such a grace,
"To play with your stick I am half mad,
    So come with me to a certain place."
The drummer out of the ranks did fall,
Being always ready at *roll call,*
And in a grove of olives thick
She play'd with the drummer's magic stick.

'Twas, &c.

The cobbler's wife came next. oh dear,
    And on the grass did quickly fall;
She said that she did feel so queer,
    Because the snob had lost his all.
Says the drummer, if that is the case,
His *awl* I quickly can replace.
He shew'd it her—says she, "how thick,
What awl can match a large drum stick?"

'Twas, &c.

The tailor's wife was fill'd with grief,
    And did her sad lot much deplore;
Her husband, to give her relief,
    Had not given her his needle for a
        month or more.
With her the drummer commenced his
    Drumming,
When she beheld her husband coming;
He came upon them in the nick,
And found her having the drummer's stick.

'Twas, &c.

Therewas three old maids, tho' fond of fun,
    Declar'd they'd never had a man,
They to the drummer off did run,
    And said they, "please us you only can."
So he laid them all upon the grass,
Brought forth the magic stick, alas!
They look'd at it till fit to burst,
Then had a mill which should have it first,

'Twas, &c.

19

Ge ho Dobin.

Within Compass of the German Flute.

Vivace — As I was a driving my Waggon one Day, I met a young Damsel tight buxom and gay, I kindly accosted her with a low Bow, and I felt my whole Body I cannot tell how. Ge ho Dobin, hi ha Dobin, Ge ho Ge Dobin Ge ho Ge ho.

Sym

A Regular Rummy Smutty Ditty, never before Printed.

Air—GEE-UP, DOBBIN.

O listen awhile, and I'll not keep you long,
I've a comical *tale* for a comical song.
To the ladies I give it, I'll tell you for why,
I know they're all fond of a *tail* on the sly.
    Tolderol, &c.

As fish is my theme, of a *maid* I will sing,
Who was sent out one day for to purchase some ling,
But, when got to the shop, she looked sad and demure,
For she could not remember what she was sent for.
    Tolderol &c.

In vain she endeavoured to think of the name,
While the fishmonger sought for to do the same,
And at first he thought he had got it, egod,
So he asked her, quite bold, if she didn't want *cod*.
    Tolderol, &c.

" O no," said the girl, " you have not yet hit it ;
For I'm so used to cod, I could never forget it."
Then the fishmonger named all the fish he thought would
Be the right ; but in vain ; neither guess it they could.
    Tolderol, &c.

At last, quite impatient, the girl said, " my
    swell,
Do you think you could guess the right fish
    by the smell ?"
" O yes, that I could," said the man, " my
    sweet maid,
'Cause I know all the arts and the rigs of my
    trade."
                  Tolderol, &c.

Then the girl shoved her hand 'neath her
    clothes, in a shot,
And rubbed it about on a certain sweet
    spot;
Then, blushing so sweetly, as you may sup-
    pose,

She put her hand up to the fishmonger's
    nose.
                  Tolderol, &c.

The fishmonger smelt it, and cried, with
    delight,
"I know what you want, by the smell, now,
    all right,
'Twas a good thought of yours, recollection
    to bring ;
I'll tell you directly—you wanted some *ling*."
                  Tolderol, &c.

—◆—

PADDY WHACK

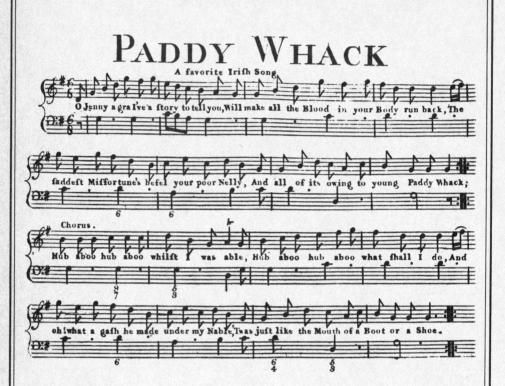

A favorite Irish Song

O Jenny a gra I've a story to tell you, Will make all the Blood in your Body run back, The saddest Misfortune's befel your poor Nelly, And all of its owing to young Paddy Whack;

Chorus.

Hub aboo hub aboo whilst I was able, Hub aboo hub aboo what shall I do, And oh! what a gash he made under my Nable, Twas just like the Mouth of a Boot or a Shoe.

A famous new Amatory Ditty.

AIR—Paddy Whack.

Young William threw Margery down on
the floor,
And with his stout gimblet began for to
bore,
But in the midst of his fibbing, and fumbling,
and thumbing,
"By my old smock," cries she, "there is
somebody coming."

But William kept driving, he was not
afraid.
Half dying with anguish, poor Margery
said,
"O lor, deary me, how you're stuffing and
strumming,
There's a foot on the stairs—there is somebody coming."

"O no," said young William, "you're mis-
taken, I'm sure,
For you know that two sentries I placed at
the door."
"By my conscience," said Madge, "you're
only a humming,
I tell you again there is somebody coming."

Not abashed still, young William kept driving away,
And teased her so much with his amorous
play,
That nature's soft stream flowed without any
humming,
"There—I told you," says she, "there was
somebody coming."

—∾—

Bonnie laddie, Highland laddie.

CHARLES WALKER.

Where ha'e ye been a' the day, Bon-nie lad-die, Highland lad-die? Saw ye him that's

far a-way, Bon-nie lad-die, High-land lad-die? On his head a bon-net blue,

Bon-nie lad-die, High-land lad-die; Tar-tan plaid and Highland trew, Bon-nie lad-die,

High-land lad-die!

A Slap-up Stave.—Air—*Bonnie Laddie.*

" Tell me, what is that I spy,
 Frisky Johnny, randy Johnny,
Hanging down beside your thigh,
 Frisky Johnny, randy Johnny?
Have you got a swelling there,
 Frisky, &c.?
You've met some accident, I fear,
 Frisky, &c."
" That lump, my love, which you now see,
 Pretty Molly, lovely Molly,
Is a prize I've got for thee,
 Pretty, &c.
It is a gem of endless worth,
 Pretty Molly, &c.
Yields the greatest bliss on earth.
 Pretty, &c.

It's round and long, with moss 'tis spread,
 Pretty, &c.
And just like coral is its head,
 Pretty, &c.
To press it, many a lass hath griev'd,
 Pretty, &c.
It must be seen to be believ'd,
 Pretty, &c.

It was old Adam's staff of life,
 Pretty, &c.
The root he planted in his wife,
 Pretty, &c.
And from that magic root, you know,
 Pretty, &c.
So many other plants did grow.'
 Pretty, &c.

Molly, pleas'd at what he said,
 Frisky Johnny, &c.
Begg'd that she might feel its head,
 Frisky, &c.

Johnny soon gave his consent,
 Frisky, &c.
So her hand into his breeches went,
 Frisky, &c.

She felt his treasure o'er and o'er,
 Frisky, &c.
And felt as she never felt before,
 Frisky, &c.
And while she finger'd it about,
 Frisky, &c.
It got so uneasy, it popp'd out,
 Frisky, &c.

Oh, how Moll feasted her eyes,
 Frisky, &c.
Admir'd its form, its make, its size,
 Frisky, &c.
So Johnny said, with a lecherous grin,
 Frisky, &c.
"As you *popt* it out, you must pop it *in*,
 Frisky, &c."

Molly blush'd, said with much grace,
 Frisky, &c.
" I would, but cannot find a place,"
 Frisky, &c.
Says John, " if that is all, my dear,
 Lovely Molly, &c.
I'll find one for you, never fear."
 Lovely, &c.

With that, within a bower, he,
 Frisky, &c.
Pull'd up Mell's clothes above her knee,
 Frisky, &c.
He roll'd about her form so plump,
 Frisky, &c.
And Moll soon brought down Johnny's
 lump,
  Frisky, &c.

The Flea Shooter

A capital new smutty Ditty, never before Printed.

AIR—London Signs.

A cobbler I am, and I once was a lodger
With a man and his wife, a regular codger,
Who had a young daughter, so tempting to view,
Who was ripe for the spit, as I very well knew.

I slept in a room next to where she reposed,
But thought of her charms all the time that I dozed,
And she was uneasy, I found without doubt,
For her amorous wishes she oft would sigh out ;

So, hot with my passion, a hole, on the sly,
I made in the wainscot, through which I could espy
When she was bed (I scarce knew what to do),
All her luscious young beauties exposed to the view.

Oh, heavens ! what transport did then fill my veins,
When I saw her quite naked, with amorous pains.
Such a belly, such thighs,—O such a pair were ne'er seen,
And a black little cuckoo's nest, right in between !

Sometimes she would wash herself over so fair,
Sometimes she would curl up her pretty black hair,
Sometimes, for a genuine grinding she groaned,
And sometimes she dildoed herself till she swooned.

One night, to my sorrow, I heard her loud cries,
Which filled me with terror as well as surprise,

When her mother came into my room in a fright,
And begged that I'd fly to her daughter with might.

"O doctor, O doctor," she cried, " pray make haste,
My daughter's so bad, you have no time to waste,
I really quite blush at her unhappy lot,
But she's got something in her poor——— you know what !"

I went to her chamber without more delay,
And what I beheld put me in a queer way ;
For there lay the lass, stretched out on the bed,
With her petticoats tumbled right over her head.

"O doctor," she cried, " I am mad, I declare,
A flea has just crept up my crevice so fair,
It drives me near crazy, he tickles me so about,
I'm sure I shall die, if I cant't get it out."

Her mother and father I bade leave the room,
Then out I pulled Roger, and that very soon.
"O sir ! What is that ?" she cried with alarm.
Said I, " It's my flea shooter. 'Twill do you no harm."

In less than a shake I was locked in her arms.
I rumbled and tumbled and rifled her charms,
Till nature prevailed, and she sighed out,
" My spark,
Ah, you've shot the flea ! What an excellent mark !"

From that happy hour, whenever she's queer,
Her illness my flea shooter's sure to repair.
So, young men, be sure, if a maid you'd delight,
Your pocket flea shooter will set her all right.

ALLEGRETTO.

Oh! 'tis Love 'tis love 'tis love that makes the World go round. Here to day, then flown a...way, For ev?.....ry where he's found. What makes the charm...ing maid more fair, Whose smiles you would obtain, What makes the faith...ful heart despair When her's it can not gain? What makes the Warrior bold, To sigh for Ro...sy Bow'rs? En...

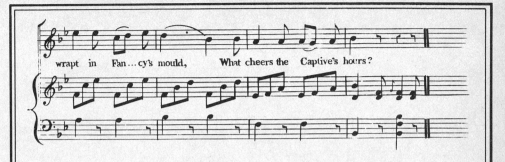

wrapt in Fan...cy's mould, What cheers the Captive's hours?

O that I in love, in love,
  In love bad never fell ;
I've tried in wain the heart to gain
  Of lovely Cats'-meat Nell.
'Twas in Drury lane, vere I
  First heard her woice so sweet,
As vith her barrow she vent by.
  And sveetly squalled " Cats'-meat !'
My heart she von ; her swivel eyes
  So charmingly she roll'd,
And tempting her vith " Pies,hot pies !"
  My tale of love I told.
    O that I in love, &c.

Elewated vith liquor, I felt no dread,
  And thought as how I'd buss her,
For vich I catch'd a lick of the head,
  Vich made me summut the vorsser.
I look'd for I felt so stupid, do you see,
  To know vhere I vas, in vain.
To a butcher says I, " I'm in Queer-
    street." Says he,
  " Why, you calf, this here is Cow-
    lane."
    O that I, &c.

I never know'd, in all my life,
  Faint heart fair lass e'er von,
So I, to try hard for a vife,
  Vith Nell again begun.
" Give me (said I) von kind embrace."
  Says she, " it's all a farce,
But, if you will kiss, kiss away ;"
And she cock'd up her bare arse.
    O that I, &c.

Says I, " Nell, I'm in love, my dear,
  And wish to know if vether
We to St. Giles's church shall steer,
  And there be spliced together."
Says she, " Mr. Pieman, it's no go,
  Vith me to talk of love,
A stinking pieman, you must know,
  I thinks myself above."
    O that I, &c.

To Holborn then away jogg'd ve,
  Vhen I ax'd her to stop.
Says I, " Nell, tho' you don't love me,
  Mayhaps you'd love a drop.
This here's The Bell, so let's toll in."
  Says she, " yer gallous polite."
And there ve took imperial gin,
  Till ve got muzzy quite.
    O that I, &c.

Close by her side I vent on, toddling,
  And, hot with love, kept chaffing,
While Nelly, vith her barrow vaddling,
  Set all the boys a laughing.
The bother of those saucy brats
  Confus'd and cross'd our cries,
So, vhile I call'd out, ' hot mutton cats,'
  Vhy Nell she bawl'd ' cats' pies !'
    O that I, &c.

An original flash Parody on
He'll no more March again.

Bob Miles, the whoremonger so bold,
　Has now lost all his meat,
With which he used to stuff the mots,
　That turf up Cockspur street.
To him the frisky little whore
　May show her notch in vain,
For, now he's lost his lump of meat,
　He'll never, never grind again.
　　　　　He'll no more grind, &c.

A kid, he bolted from his home
　(A gallows rogue was he),
With red-haired Moll, the fat a—e mot,
　He soon was a C. P.

His fame for grinding quickly spread,
　His Roger caused sad pain,
But it's rotted off with the woful p—,
　And he'll never grind again.
　　　　　He'll no more, &c.

A jock, so strong as Billy's was,
　The blowen's heart would cheer,
And when she now beholds his stump,
　She drops a briny tear ;
And red-haired Moll, his sole delight,
　Chief blowen of the train,
Rubs up her precious Fan., and cries,
　" Poor Bill will never grind you again."
　　　　　He'll never more, &c.

32

Mrs. Bond

There un _der the Bow'r on ro _ ses you'll lie, with a blush on your

cheek but a smile in your eye, there un _der the Bow'r in ro _ ses you'll

lie with a blush on your cheek but a smile in your eye Will you will you

will you will you smile my beloved will you will you will you will you smile my be _

loved

A right-down rummy Ditty, never before
Printed, and Sung at all the Select
Convivial Meetings.

AIR—Will you come to the Bower?

Oh, I'm getting still more hot for you, my
    charming Mrs. Bond,
And though you will not smile on me, I never
    will despond.
This moment, when I write to you, indeed
    quite stiff I stand,
And—all that I possess, is sweating in my
    hand.
    Then won't you let me, won't you let me
    —tickle you, Mrs Bond?
    Even randy little duchesses have lured
    me to their arms,
    And crumby little countesses have yiel-
    ded me their charms.
Then, only give me leave to go a fishing
    in your pond,
I've got a rod so long and strong, and
    such fine bait, Mrs. Bond.

Every morning I view you at your toilette,
    when you rise,
And watch the towel's motion, as you wash
    your lovely thighs.
I pray for some enchantress, to transform
    me with her wand,
To the chamber pot you hold betwixt your
    thighs, sweet Mrs. Bond.
If the gods would grant my wishes, and ac-
    complish my request,
I'd seek to be a flea, to skip upon your
    breast,

Or, I'd pray to be a petticoat, of flannel or
    of blond,
To chafe your panting belly and your bub-
    bies, Mrs. Bond.
        Then won't you, &c.

At eve I seek the privy, which your presence
    may have blest,
And kiss the very timber which your lilly
    duff has prest.
Even the very paper on which I write this
    billet-doux,
It is gilt-edge, you see, by being s—t upon
    by you.
Even in my sleep I hourly am attacked.
My laundress and my night shirt can tstifye
    the fact.
My passions are so hot and so exquisitely
    fond,
My very f——ts I ave learned to trump the
    praise of Mrs. Bond.
        Then won't you, &c.

Mrs. Bond, you must forgive me, but indeed
    I cannot wait,
So you'd better ope your pretty mouth, and
    swallow all my bait.
There's one reflection left, to solace me be-
    yond,
I'll never go a fishing, if it's not in your
    pond.
    Then won't you let me, won't you let me—
    tickle you, Mrs. Bond?
    Won't you let me, won't you let me—go a
    fishing in your pond?
        J. H. L.

35

Come Sleep with Me

COME DWELL WITH ME.

Poetry by T. H. Bayly Esq:

Composed by Alexander Lee.

ANDANTE.

Come dwell, come dwell with me And our home shall be, our

home shall be A pleasant cot, in a tranquil spot, With a distant view of the

changing sea; My cottage is a magic scene, The shelt'ring boughs seem ever

Air—"*Come dwell with me.*"

Come, sleep with—come, snooze with me—
And our bed shall be, our bed shall be,
A pleasant place that's in King's Place,
Where I'll shew you my jewel case.
I've got a treasure you've ne'er seen,
And you've a spot that it will screen;
'Twill please you when in bed we be,
And then we'll plough the deep deep C.
                    Come, &c.

The little secret gem of mine,
Around that secret spot of thine,
With pleasure I will then entwine,
And you will own it quite divine.
I will not make you once regret
You slept with me, my slap-up Bet;
'Twill be my pride to hear thee say—
Come, with my little crevice play.
                    Come, &c.

—⁊—

38

The Blue Bells of Ireland

Sung at all the Slap-up Free and Easies.

NEWS, neighbours, news, glorious news I've
    to tell,
Here's a waggon-load of patent beetroots
    come here to sell,
And if you'll be my customers, by gosh I'll
    use you well!
    And the blue bells of Ireland go well,
        boys, well,
    And the clapper strikes on every side,
        bang young Fanny well!

In came a lady gay, the footman ran be-
    fore,
Desiring that she might have one nine inches
    long—no more,
And when Johnny touched her Fanny up,
    she still cried encore!
            And the, &c.

In came the parson's wife, as demure as you
    please,
And she would have a little one, to give
    herself some ease,
For parson's beet-root, while a-preaching,
    dangled to his knees.
            And the, &c.

In came a gardener's wife, and she was
    clothed in green,

And in buying of a dozen, she stole away
    fifteen,
And crammed them in her hairy pouch, that
    they might not be seen.
            And the, &c.

In came the vintner's wife, and she was full
    of spleen,
And she would have the largest that ever yet
    was seen,
For she had been plagued with little ones,
    e'er since she was fifteen.
            And the, &c.

In came the sailor's wife, and she was from
    Blackwall,
She bought a waggon load of roots, the wag-
    goner and all,
To make amends for loss of time, while Jack
    was at Bengal.
            And the, &c.

The next there came a little miss, resolved
    to play her part,
And when she heard the roots were sold, I
    thought 'twould break her heart.
" Pray, give me leave," says she, " to rub
    my Fanny 'gainst your cart !"
            And the, &c.

Blythe have I been on you hill.

Allegretto

Blythe have I been on yon hill As the Lambs be_fore me; Care_lefs il_ka

thought and free As the breeze flew o'er me Now nae langer sport and play, Or

mirth or sang can please me; LESLEY is sae fair and coy, Care and anguish seize me.

A capital new Smutty Stave.

AIR—Merrily Danced the Quaker's Wife.

Young Ellen Lovecock was a lass
　　Both beautiful and tender,
There warn't a lad in all the town
　　Who'd willingly offend her.
But though she was but just fifteen,
　　And humble was her station,
Each night as she lay on her bed,
　　She felt—such a queer sensation.
　　　　　　　　Tooral lal loo, &c.

Young Lubin he was stout and strong,
　　And kissed her more than one day;
He used to walk her in the fields,
　　But that was every Sunday.
One day, while wandering through　a
　　　　grove,
　　In a state of agitation,
He slipped his hand above her knee,
　　For he felt such a queer sensation.
　　　　　　　　Tooral, &c.

43

Young Ellen blushed like any rose,
    But O, she couldn't resist him.
His fingers wandered 'neath her clothes,
    And, filled with joy, she kissed him.
While pressed unto her belly tight,
    His roger left his station,
And stood revealed before her sight,
    While she felt such a queer sensation.
                      Tooral, &c.

Then down they both sunk on the grass
    Lubin till now had felt it,
But Ellen's petticoats flew up,
    And of course he then beheld it.
The sight increased his lecherous fire.
    She cried, in consternation,
" O Lubin, Lubin, I expire,
    I feel such a queer sensation."
                      Tooral, &c.

Four times they played their amorous
             sport,
    Till nature could no longer.
Then Ellen sighed, " O would, my dear,
    That roger was but stronger !"
But, after all, indeed it's true,
    Whate'er our rank and station,
Young Roger is the only thing
    To cure a queer sensation.
                      Tooral, &c.

He Did it before my Face

A regular rummy Song, now first Printed.

AIR—He was such a Nice Young Man.

One day, as I was walking out,
  And crossing o'er the plain,
I suddenly beheld, O dear,
  A very handsome swain;
And while I looked at him about,
  And viewed his manly grace,
A certain member he pulled out,—
  He did, before my face!

Transfixed I was unto the spot,
  Of that you may be sure,
For such a curious instrument
  I never saw before;
And while I looked upon its size,
  In my hand he it did place,
And felt the secret charms I had,—
  He did, before my face.

Now on the grass, where daisies spread,
  And decked the spot around,
He clasped my waist, and then he placed
  Me gently on the ground.
Then down he pulled his buckskins new,
  And commenced his amorous race,
And dangled two large apples too,—
  He did, before my face.

Transported with our mutual joys,
  We kissed six times or more.
I could not tell him to be still,—
  No fault of mine, I'm sure.
But sure he was no hypocrite,
  And therefore no disgrace,
For, whate'er he did, I can't deny,—
  He did before my face!

The Magic Crab-Tree

AIR—Umbrella Courtship.

The moon was shining bright above,
  No darkening cloud did shade her,
When Susan, full of youth and love,
  In loose attire arrayed her.
The twinkling stars enticed her out,
  And she decoyed her sister,
And many a lustful youth so stout,
  Would have died could he but kissed her.
    Ri fol, &c.

Inclined for mirth, thus Susan said,
  " Come here dear sister Chloe,
I've learned to stand upon my head,
  As I will quickly show ye."
Then she did what she said she could do,
  dear, 'twas quite alarming,
For, quite exposed unto the view
  Was her little grot so charming.
    Ri fol, &c.

To steal the pears upon a tree
  Close by, a youth was mounted,
And at the sight he then did see,
  In bliss he was quite drowned.

Her charms of course were all undrest,
  And the grot, between her haunches,
Resembled much a magpie's nest
  Between two lofty branches.
    Ri fol, &c.

In this inviting posture stood
  The lady near a minute.
Jack took the choicest fruit he could,
  And fairly threw them in it.
It soon took root, the soil being fine,
  Indeed the truth I tell ye;
And, from that hour, the damsel had
  A crab-tree in her belly!
    Ri fol, &c.

In pleasing shades the stalks arose,
  And ranged themselves in order,
And where the bubbling fountain flows,
  Hang wavering o'er its border.
The men all came to graft the same,
  And sported 'tween the haunches.
She liked to let them plant their tree
  Between her lovely branches.
    Ri fol, &c.

*A famous new smutty Recitation, given with
Thunders of Applause at all Select
Meetings,*

And never before in Print.

List to my tale, it is a merry one,
And will just suit all those who're fond of
  fun,
'Tis true indeed, and that I soon shall
  show,
Though it occurred some centuries ago.
Well, to be brief, once on a time, a friar,
As fat a soul as one could well desire,
To wash his hands unto a river sped,
And there his eyes beheld a lovely maid,
With all her charms exposed to view, alas !
And in the river washing clean her a—e.

Filled with hot passions, then, this holy
  friar,
With greedy looks did long and wistful eye
  her,
But what amazed him, let the truth be said,
Was that her backside was so very red.
Long, long he viewed her, wishing to caress
  her,
And then approximating, thus he did address
  her,
" My pretty lass, I pray be not in dread,
But tell me why your buttocks look so red."

The maid, quite pert, as many maidens be,
Replied unto his question wittily,
" Why, holy friar, the reason I'll soon tell,
But pay attention, and now mark me well.
The reason is, my backside looks so red,
With carrying fire in Fan, to warm my mas-
  ter's bed."
" If that's the case," the friar then replied,
And then his girdle he so quick untied,
And bringing forth a s'aft as big as he could
  handle,
" Pray give me leave," said he, " to light
  this candle."

The maid complied, and granted his request
And in five minutes made the friar blest,
And very quickly, with her lecherous play,
She melted all his tal ow then away,
Until, to prove that he had had enough,
His Roman candle she brought to a snuff,
Then down the friar knelt upon the ground,
And looking at her Fanny, quite profound,
" Lighten my darkness," he exclaimed, de-
  vout,
" For, upon my soul, my candle's quite
  burnt out."

46

Colin and Susan

A famous New Smutty Song.

Air—THE UMBRELLA COURTSHIP.

'Twas on a summer's night, O dear,
  That, far away from home,
Susan the milkmaid did repair
  To the meadows with young Tom.
As they tripped it light, along,
  Tom felt in such a glow,
He longed to—do a certain thing ;
  But she said, " No, No, No!"

" Oh, you cruel maid," said Tom,
  " My passion to defy !
You've set my blood in such a glow,
  I'm certain I shall die ;
Only just taste a little bit,
  You needn't swallow all, you know.
Besides, there's no one here to see !
  Shall I ?"—Still 'twas " No, No, No !"

Thus they walked up to a hill,
  Which Tom, so frisky, raced her down ;
But, luckless maid, her foot it slipped,
  And all her little charms were shown.
Tom could not this sight resist ;
  But by her side himself did throw,
And put a something in her fist ;
  But still she answered, " No, No, No !"

" Oh, get you gone !" the damsel cried,
  This monstrous form fills me with dread ;
And what would mother say," she sighed,
  " If I should lose my maidenhead ?"
" You silly girl," the swain replied,
  " To praise you she could not be slow ;
For, I'm sure, if she saw one like this,
  She would not answer " No, No, No!"

Susan now grew still more tender,
  As Colin's treasure met her sight ;
Half inclined to surrender,
  And in his arms to seek delight.
Colin saw her, panting, throbbing,
  And in his arms her form did press ;
And when she once had tasted Robin,
  Her tune was changed to " Yes, yes, yes!"

After the first round was done,
  Susan, panting, longing, lay ;
And said, " I do so like the fun,
  I wish at it you'd once more play !"
Full six times they'd it in clover,
  And Susan really liked it so,
She fairly tired Colin over,
  Who was forced to cry out " No, No, No!"

The Bower that Stands in Thigh Lane

Printed by G. Bown, Music Seller, No. 11 St Martin's Church Yard.

Och!

Love is the Soul of a neat Irishman He loves all that's lovely, loves all that he can, With his

Sprig of Shillelah and Shamrock so green   His

heart is good humour'd 'tis honest and sound No malice or hatred is there to be found He

courts and he marries He drinks & he fights For love all for love for in that he delights with his

Sprig of Shillelah and Shamrock so green

48

A capital smutty Song, now first printed.

AIR—"*Sprig of Shilalah.*"

Young Bessy had bloom'd to the age of fif-
teen,
When she felt a strange itching and tickling
between
    That sweet little spot that is close to thigh
    lane;
So one day quite uneasy she lay on her bed,
When a comical thought it came into her
head ;
So she pull'd up her shift, and then, I de-
clare,
A bower so thick to her eyes did appear,
    At the top of that spot that stands in thigh
    lane.

Now Bessy had heard that the men were all
mad
To *stand* in her bower—that would make
them glad—

For 'twas a sweet pretty bower, the one in
thigh lane.
She had heard of a pleasure, and something
she guess'd
By their towzing and tumbling, and pressing
her breast,
She saw the men eager, but was at a loss
What they meant then by pinching and
squeezing so close
    Her neat little bower that stood in thigh
    lane.

Daily poor Bessy more uneasy grew,
Till she wriggled and really knew not what
to do,
    For the bushes had grown so around by
    thigh lane.
She knew she must die, as she oft did de-
clare,
If her bower was not quickly put in repair;

But though at the entrance the men their
   time *spent*,
A'las! oh, she never could guess what they
   meant
   By their sneaking so close to the bower in
   thigh lane.

One day a young gard'ner, so neat and so
   clean,
By chance came that way while she slept in
   the green,
   And he twigg'd her sweet bower at the
   top of thigh lane.
With bushes and briars being quite over-
   grown,
Says he —"'tis a pity, and that all must own.'
So as Bessy lay there, just like any Turk,
He pull'd forth his rake and quick went to
   work
   At the sweet little bower at the top of
   thigh lane.

Bessy, woke up with his amorous wiles,
And with her face clad with blushes, wishes,
   and smiles,
   She found a good workman not far from
   thigh lane.

He handled his rake with such skill and such
   might,
Poor Bessy did very near faint with delight,
Till the entrance was open and let in the air,
And the water ran smooth, and so rapid, and
   clear,
   Through the sweet little bower at the top
   of thigh lane.

"Sweet youth (then she said), since your
   tool works so free,
In future the gard'ner you're welcome to be,
   Of the neat little bower at top of thigh
   lane.
The swain took the hint, and from that very
   day,
Every morning in Bessy's bower he works
   away;
He's turned up the ground, and he's
   planted a *root*,
That gives notice it soon will produce some
   rare fruit
   In the neat little bower at top of thigh
   lane.

The New Rolling Pin

AIR—Derry Down.

Young Polly was told by her mother one
day,
That she had invited a party so gay
On the morrow; and so she desired she'd
make
A pudding, so rich it their fancy should
take,

Now Polly, although she seemed none of
the sort,
Was decidedly fond of the amorous sport,
So her mother she told, their favour to win,
She must have for her pudding a new roll-
ing pin.

She went to a shop then, to buy one with
speed,
And a very good rolling pin it was indeed.
But Poll fixed her eye on the shopman's tall
form,
And wished he might take her sly fortress
by storm.

The youth took the hint, followed her with
a sigh,
And popt in the kitchen to her on the sly,
And quickly the damsel his favour did win,
To see how she handled the new rolling pin.

" My darling," said she, in manner so pat,
" I've a rolling pin that's still better than
that.

It will roll it and troll it, and bread out your
dough."
" Oh, have you ?" said she, " the same
pr'ythee show."
The youth, not abashed, not deeming it
wrong,
A something exhibited, twelve inches long.
" O my !" said young Polly, and that with
a grin,
" I should much like to **try** your new rolling
pin !"

Then down on the dresser young Polly he
laid,
And having with rapture love's altar sur-
veyed,
He thought it was time he the fun should
begin,
So he kneaded her dough with his new rolling pin.

With many soft kisses they parted, they say.
Says Polly, " You're welcome to call every
day.
But as my puddings no doubt general favour
will win,
Never come here without your new rolling
pin.

51

ALLEGRO.

VOCE

PIANO

FORTE.

My

love was born in A—ber—deen, The bonniest lad that e'er was seen, But

now he make sae hearts fu' sad, He takes the field wi' his white cockade.

Oh! he's a ranting, roving lad, he is a brisk an' a bonny lad, Be—

tide what may, I will be wed, And follow the boy wi' the white cockade.

54

A famous new smutty ditty never before
Printed

Air—*The White Cockade.*

In London town not long ago,
A laundress lived as you must know,
Who had a daughter young and fair,
Whose beauty made the male sex queer.
Now Betty was a clever maid,
And help'd her mother at her trade,
'Till one day with grief I tell the quick,
Her mother lost the copper stick,
It was such a rummy copper stick.
A long, a strong, good copper stick,
An instrument to do the trick,
But alas! she lost the copper stick.

All round about did Betty look,
In every corner, every nook,
But vain her search fate was unkind,
The copper stick she could not find.

Up stairs ran Bet to escape the route,
And from the window she peep'd out;
When underneath the little miss,
A youth came up and began to p—ss!
He show'd a member long and thick,
A regular one to do the trick,
And Betty who saw it cried out quick,
" By jingo that's my mother's copper stick.

Just like a shot down stairs she flew,
And the street door wide open threw,
And catching hold of the man quite cool,
Pull'd him into the hall by his lanky tool.
Says she my mother has lost, oh dear,
A copper stick, I do declare,
But as we're going to wash to morrow,
This here for a copper stick I'll borrow.
It is so very long and thick,
Just the sort to do the trick,
May every woman—when in the nick,
Always find such a funny copper stick.

AIR—There's nae Luck.

Bet Mild she was a servant maid,
  And she a place had got,
To wait upon two ladies fair
  These ladies' name was Scott.
Now Bet a certain talent had,
  For she any thing could handle,
And for these ladies, every night,
  She used a large thick candle.

So push, push, shove, shove,
  Drive away with all your might.
Push, push, shove, shove,
  'Tis that that yields delight.

Althouh these ladies modest seemed,
  In truth they only mocked,
Pretending, if they saw a man,
  Their modesty was shocked.
In fact, these wantons thought it best,

As it would smother scandal,
To use, instead of the real thing,
  A cobbler's twopenny candle.
                              So push, &c.

Now Betty had a sweetheart got,
  It was their footman Ned,
Who slipped into their room one night,
  And crept beneath the bed;
And there he saw them at the fun,
  As he his tool did dandle.
Says he, " I'll give to them a thing
  Much better than the candle."
                              Push, &c.

So Ned he made poor Betty drunk,
  Then took her in his arms,
Carried her up stairs to bed,
  And rifled all her charms.
Then all her toggery he put on,
  Her shift, her shoes, her sandal,

57

And underneath his clothes, of course,
  Was his long Roman candle.
            Push, &c.

He being dressed, looked like the maid,
  Went to the ladies' bed,
And very soon the ladies came,
  But little thought 'twas Ned.
Into the bed they quickly got,
  And very soon did handle
Something more stiff, and stouter too,
  Than any cobbler's candle.
            Push, &c.

Fainting with joy, the ladies cried,
  " Why, Betty, how is this ?
You never used a candle yet,
  That yielded us such bliss.
I'm sure it must be melted quite,
  The wick come let us handle."
So Ned complied with what they wished,
  And gave to them more candle.
            Push, &c.

When in the morning Ned get up,
  He to his Betty went.
She little thought her place usurped,
  Or what a night he'd spen'.
Says she to him, " I'm with child,
  " To me 'twill be a scandal."
" O never mind, my love," says Ned,
  " It's all owing to the candle."
            Push, &c.

The ladies both swelled round the waist,
  And so did Betty Mild.
" O dear," said they to Betty, then,
  " I fear we're all with child."
A few months more, the truth came out,
  Likewise three little Randles.
So, ladies, all a warning take.
  Ne'er play with Roman candles!
            Push, &c.

There is no Shove like the First Shove

THERE'S NO LOVE LIKE THE FIRST LOVE.

Written by J. E. CARPENTER. ◄◄◄►►► Composed by E. J. LODER.

AFFETTUOSO.

They tell me to for-get him, And I strive to think I do; When the heart he should have cherish'd An-other comes to woo..... But I vain-ly try to banish All the pleasant dreams of youth. But I

vain-ly try to banish All the plea-sant dreams of youth. Oh there's

no love like the first love, For con-stan-cy and truth. Oh there's

no love like the first love, For con-stan-cy and truth........

An entire new amorous Parody on

There is no **Love** like the first **Love.**

Though randy coves may bluster,
  And talk a precious lot
Of the pleasures they experience
  Every night with some old mot,
Let them grind them, if they like it,
  But my belief is this,
There is no shove like the first shove,
  For ecstasy and bliss.

When a girl's just turned sixteen,
  And of beauty she does smack,
O is it not a pleasure, then,
  Her little notch to crack,
To lay her on her duff, then,
  And her belly white to kiss?

At the first shove, if 'tis a good shove,
  Won't she swoon away with bliss?

O the transport of that moment,
  I can't describe, I'm sure,
It must be such joy to her
  Who has ne'er seen a jock before.
But when she feels its large nose,
  And trembles out, " What's this?"
O there's no shove like the **first** shove,
  For ecstasy and bliss.

Then give to me a maiden,
  Whose door is tight as air,
With my master key so tempting,
  I'll soon make an entry there.
I'd go to work with transport,
  For my belief is this,
There is no shove like the first shove,
  For ecstasy and bliss !

The Way to Come over a Maid

A laughable bawdy Song, now first printed.

Air—*Bob and Joan.*

If you'd get over a maid,
　Tickle and amuse her;
Any thing she asks,
　Mind you ne'er refuse her.
Walk her out each day,
　O'er the fields romantic;
Roll her in the hay,
　With many a lustful antic.
　　　　　　Tol de rol, &c.

First her bubbies feel,
　To raise her hot desire;
Next just feel her thigh,
　Then a little higher!
If she won't wince at that,
　Put Bob in her grasp then;
And depend when it she feels,
　She'll take a precious rasping!
　　　　　　Fol de rol, &c.

If she simpers "oh!"
　Embrace her, then caress her;
Disrobe her form below,
　Entwine round her and press her!
Soon you'll find her yield,
　For her lust gets stronger;
One more close embrace,
　And she's a maid no longer!
　　　　　　Fol de rol, &c.

But if a widow you'd kiss,
　You must be much bolder;
For as they've sipt the bliss,
　They don't feel much the colder!
If you'd seduce a maid,
　You must swear, and sigh, and flatter,
But if you'd win a widow,
　You must down with your breeches and
　　　at her!
　　　　　　Fol de rol, &c.

61

O'er the water to Charlie.

187

Come boat me o'er, come row me o'er, Come boat me o'er to

Lively

Charlie; I'll gie John Ross another bawbee, To boat me o'er to Charlie.

We'll o'er the water, we'll o'er the sea, We'll o'er the water to Charlie; Come

weal, come woe, we'll gather and go, And live or die wi' Charlie.

A rum randy chaunt, now first printed.

Air—"Over the water to Charlie."

A jolly Jack-tar was benighted one night,
  And as through the wood he was dodging,
A merry old farmer by chance hove in sight,
  Of whom he enquired for a lodging;
The farmer replied, with a cheerful good will,
  Though a home very humble I'm keeping,
If you'll go to my house, and inform my good
    wife,
  She'll provide you with victuals and sleeping.
          Tol de rol, &c.

The tar thank'd the farmer, who told him the way,
  Then they quickly shook daddles and parted;
To meet with such luck the Jack-tar was quite
    gay,
  So away to the cottage he started.
He quickly arrived there, and knock'd at the
    door,
  The farmer's wife came to behold him;
So she asked him his business, and then, in a
    trice,

He said what the farmer had told him.
          Tol de rol, &c.

Now it happen'd that she was a lecherous dame,
  And this message she did not much relish,
For whenever the farmer was out, to her came
  The parson, so gay, of the parish!
So at what the tar said, as you all may suppose,
  She look'd half as dingy as sable;
However, being willing the business to close,
  She said he might sleep in the stable!
          Tol de rol, &c.

The tar being tired, accepted the same,
  And the stable he soon popt his head in;
Where he raked up the straw in a heap, to be sure,
  And quickly got into his bedding.
But scarce had he been there, when he heard a
    great noise—
  A sighing, a wriggling, and shaking;
So he peep'd through a hole in the wall, and he
    saw
  What sat him with laughter a aching!
          Tol de rol, &c.

Down on the floor was the farmer's fair wife,
  In a state that was really quite scarish;
While a gent, dress'd in black, was a toying away,
  Whom he guess'd was the parson of th' parish.
My eyes! cried the tar, here's a pretty affair—
  You old lubber—I'm sure he should steer baft;
In another man's birth to stow himself there—
  Here's the parson aboard of the fair craft!
            Tol de rol, &c.

The wife kiss'd the parson's red gills o'er and
    o'er,
And he slobber'd and tickled her over;
What they did once or twice, I sha'n't tell you,
    I'm sure,
But you'll guess they were both quite in clover.
At length being tired, they rested awhile,
  The parson seemed weak in the crupper;
So the female got meat and punch with a smile,
  And they both sat them down then to supper.
            Tol de rol, &c.

But their pleasure, alas! it was soon to be o'er,
  As I mean very quickly to show it;
For very soon came a loud knock at the door—
  'Tis my husband, cried dame, I well know it.
The parson's fat gills grew quite pale at this
    news,
  For he guess'd he should get a good topper;
But the dame, who'd more thought, no chance
    to lose,
  Shoved both parson and meat in the copper.
            Tol de rol, &c.

When the farmer came in he for supper enquired,
  But the dame, who with fear was near dying,
Declared she had nothing but some bread and
    cheese
  His hunger then to be supplying.
He next ask'd for the sailor, at which she look'd
    glum,
  But past it off as well as she was able;
So she told him as soon as he'd to the farm come,
  He'd gone off to sleep in the stable.
            Tol de rol, &c.

The farmer called out with a hearty halloo,
  Come, sailor—for you, to my thinking,
As well as being tired, are hungry, my tar,
  So come, and be eating and drinking.
Then the sailor appeared, and thank'd him so free,
  They sat themselves down on the chattels,
And the sailor amused the good farmer, d'ye see,
  By relating both shipwrecks and battles.
            Tol de rol, &c.

One tale brought another—the farmer enquired,
  When at sea, how it often depended,
That by hunger oppressed, and their food was
    all out,
  How they did when their food was expended.
Oh, oh, said the tar, by a few words, we say,
  Though, of victuals our stores are quite empty,
In less than a minute, by a few words we say,
  We are quickly supplied with a plenty.
            Tol de rol, &c.

How's that? said the farmer—I'll tell you, said
    Jack;
  And as we're both hungry—an evil—
I'll get a good supper, and that in a crack,
  But we first must get rid of the devil.
But that in the effort we both should not stick,
  Don't let fear ever enter your topper;
Get a pail-full of water, and then very quick
  You must pour it bang into the copper.
            Tol de rol, &c.

When this you have done, have another at hand,
  Set open the door there before him;
And when he jumps out, mind this is the plan,
  Throw the second pail likewise bang over him.
The farmer agreed—got the pail in a trice,
  Determined to carry the farce on;
Threw it into the copper, being not over nice,
  When out jumped the amorous parson.
            Tol de rol, &c.

The parson he ran, as you all may be sure,
  Jack laughed to see all done so neatly;
And the farmer, as Spinless run out from the
    door,
  Threw the second pail over him completely.
But as he run out, the farmer exclaimed,
  Why, dang it, this seems very queerish;
For if that be the devil, I vow and declare,
  He's exact like our parson o' the parish.
            Tol de rol, &c.

From the copper the sailor then took all the store,
  Meat and punch, such a quantity really;
The farmer declared that he wonder'd the more,
  Then they sat down to supper so gaily.
They enjoyed a good meal, and they laugh'd at
    the fun,
  Which many rum jokes they did pass on;
But from that day the water of cuckolding men
  It cured the old amorous parson.
            Tol de rol, &c.

A Capital New Smutty Song.

AIR—*Nothing at All.*

Ye maidens, ye wives, and young widows,
 rejoice !
Proclaim a thanksgiving with heart and with
 voice !
For from London town there has lately come
 down
Four able physicians as ever were
 known !
Many wonderful cures they have done and
 do;
Their great belly physic's unknown but to
 few ;
It's for females alone, and the dose too is
 large ;
And you may be cured without danger or
 charge.

No bolus or vomit, no potion or pill,
Which sometimes do cure, but oft'ner do
 kill,
Your taste or your stomach need never
 displease,
If you'll be advis'd but by one of these.
For they've a new drug that's call'd the
 close hug,
Which will mend your complexion and make
 you look snug ;
A sovereign basam, to the belly applied,
And shot through a pipe that has often been
 tried.

In the morning you need not be robb'd of
 your rest,
For in your warm beds the physic works
 best;
And though in the taking some stirring's
 required,

The motion's so pleasant, you cannot be
 tir'd.
On your back you must lie, with your body
 rais'd high,
And one of those doctors must ever be
 by,
Who will be ready to cover you warm,
For if you take cold, all physic doth
 harm !

Before they dare venture to give their direc-
 tion,
They always consider their patient's complexion.
If she have a moist palm, or a red head of
 hair,
She requires more physic than one man can
 spare,
If she have a long nose, the doctor scarce
 knows
How many good handfuls must go to her
 dose,
You ladies that have such ill symptoms as
 these,
In reason and conscience should pay double
 fees !

But that we may give these doctors due
 praise,
Who please various people by various
 ways,
All damsels who feel themselves in a queer
 way,
May be physick'd, and for it have nothing
 to pay !
The doctor his pipe will apply beyond mea-
 sure,
And always is willing to work for the pleasure ;
But his patients must spend a good deal, you
 must learn,
Though, unlike most doctors, he must spend
 in return.

Sally's Thatched Cottage

Air—Dumble dum deary.

In Gloucestershire, as I've heard say,
Young Roger he mounted his dobbin grey,
Then to a neighbouring village went,
To hire a cottage was his intent.
     Dumble dum deary, &c.

Now Sally a neat thatch'd cottage had,
Just suited to our country lad,
'Twas very small, but very neat,
With a little entrance quite complete.
     Dumble dum, &c.

Now Roger saw Sally's little cot,
And felt inclin'd for it, I wot.
Says she, my cottage is yours quite clear,
But the rent is just ten pounds a-year.
     Dumble dum, &c.

Roger agreed to this with joy,
And took possession without alloy,
At the end of the year he was walking away,
But says Sal, you've got your rent to pay.
     Dumble dum, &c.

Roger refused to settle; so she
Went to the magistrate, so free.
My cottage of thatch to this man I lent,
He's had it a year, and he won't pay the rent.
     Dumble dum, &c.

Roger began to give her some abuse,
And said her old cottage it was of no use.

Besides the trouble at which he had been,
To open the door when he first got in.
     Dumble dum, &c.

Sal said, of his usage to give him a proof,
He had knock'd nearly all of the thatch from
   the roof,
He'd crack'd it, and tore it a deal, I declare,
And therefore he'd left it much out of repair.
     Dumble dum, &c.

Roger declared his case was hard,
For to Sal's cottage he'd plac'd a yard;
He'd sunk a well, and dug it round,
And he'd pav'd it too with stones of his own.
     Dumble dum, &c.

Said Sal, my door was tight and close,
It scarcely would admit a mouse,
But now it opened so often has been,
A donkey might with ease get in!
     Dumble dum, &c.

The magistrate smiled, and he scratch'd his
   nob,
Then mentioned the best plan to settle the
   job,
That Roger should make little Sally his wife,
And work hard in her cottage the rest of his
   life.   Dumble dum, &c.

The Hedger and Ditcher and his Nothing at All

Air—Nothing at All.

Miss Deborah Dainty, just aged thirty-three,
Determin'd at last that she married would be,
Selected the first man that came in her way,
Which was Roger, a hedger and ditcher,
  they say.
Her thoughts were on fire the whole of the
  night,
He thought of her money, she thought of
  delight.
But, lord! the delight that came to her was
  small,
They were wed, went to bed, and did—
  nothing at all.
              Fooral, &c.

Roger snor'd like a top, though she nudg'd
  him and sighed,
And "don't you snore so," very fondly she
  cried:
Then she kissed him, and teased him with
  amorous play,
But Roger turn'd over, and still snor'd away.
Then she pinch'd him, and pull'd him, until
  he awoke,
He grumbled, while she to him thus kindly
  spoke,
" Now, pray, do, do something," " I will,"
  he did bawl.
" Ah, will ye? well, what?" " Why—do
  nothing at all."   Fooral, &c.

Now Roger still slept, and the maiden still
  whined,
And said that her spouse was to nothing
  inclined;

Then bade both the world and her plea-
  sures adieu,
Pinch'd his ribs, call'd him fool, and went
  to sleep too.
She dreamt of joy which she then did not
  feel,
And on only a vision of love made a meal,
She long'd for something, though ever so
  small,
But he, stupid lout, long'd for *nothing at all.*
              Fooral, &c.

When a week in this way they had mur-
  der'd or more,
Her wonder and passion were roused, to be
  sure ;   [pot,
And so she determin'd, what might come to
To find if he something or nothing had got.
Curiosity prompting, one night, when he
  snor'd,
The source of her sorrow she quickly ex-
  plor'd,
And saw quite enough forth her sorrow to call,
She look'd, and she look'd, and saw *nothing
  at all.*   Fooral, &c.

In despair from her husband next morning
  she fled,
And into a river jumpt souse overhead,
And there she remain'd with the fishes be-
  low,
Till death in compassion had finish'd her woe.
But her spirit, they say, has not felt sor-
  row's rod,
For courted it was by a monstrous great cod;
I cant say it's true, so the tale I'll not maul,
But I know that she died, and for—*nothing
  at all.*

The Nipple

The Nipple

Air—*The Bard's Legacy.*

As beautiful Nelly, one fine summer's mor-
ning,
  Was milking her cow on the meadow so
  green,
William the ploughman that was a-passing,
  And he gazed with delight on her fine
  graceful-mien.
Her face look'd so rosy, her bosom was
  heaving,
  Her black sparkling eye beam'd with le-
  chery bright ;
She held the cow's udder so neat and so tender,
  And pulled it and squeez'd it away with
  delight.

As William stood gazing, he felt a sensation,
  A kind of a feeling that can't be exprest ;
With his hand in his breeches to ease his
  warm feelings,
He pinch'd her plump buttocks, and thus
  her addrest :
" O Nelly, dear Nelly, why handle that
  udder,
  Which only can put you into a bad way ;
When I've got a nipple, so fine and so
  tempting,
  That would give you such pleasure, if
  with it you'd play."

Says Nelly to William, and blush'd all so
  sweetly,
  " I feel what you tell me is true to be sure ;
The feel of this udder but sets me a-longing,
  I've heard of your nipple, Bill, often be-
  fore.
And if it's so good as Dolly has told me,
  For she says she tried it last week in the
  wood ;
Oh, grant me one favor—oh, pray let me see it,
  I'd milk such a nipple, indeed that I
  would !"

William was pleased at the maid's conde-
  scension,
  And so to a bower they quickly then flew ;
As gay as a fairy, he unlock'd his dairy,
  And instantly brought forth the nipple to
  view !
Nelly delighted, seiz'd hold of it tightly,
  While the touch set the whole of her blood
  in a glow :
" Oh, William," she cries, "what a beau-
  tiful nipple,
  And, la ! here's your bubbies are hanging
  below !"

Nelly kept dandling and fondling the nipple,
  While her bosom with various emotions
    was torn ;
Till all on a sudden it grew three times larger
  And besides it was stiffer than any cow's
    horn !
She cried in surprise—" Oh, William pray
    tell me,
  The reason the nipple's so stiff and so
    queer ?
" The reason " said he, " oh, I'll tell you
    that quickly,   .
  It's only because it wants milking, my dear."

Says Nelly, " to milk it I'm sure I am wil-
    ling,
  But then, my dear William, I don't know
    the way ;"
Says William, " I'll learn you to do it di-
    rectly,
  If down on the grass, love, you will with
    me lay ! "

Quick as a shot, she lay down on her back
    then,
  And he did the same, fully bent for the
    play ;
She found out a place—just to work of the
    nipple,
  And Nelly and William went milking away.

For more than an hour she work'd at the
    nipple,
  Whose touch seem'd to her as soft as vel-
    vet or silk ;
Till William cried out—" you have work'd
    long enough, love,
  At present the dairy contains no more milk.
But meet me to-morrow, if you are but wil-
    ling,
  And I'm sure, my dear Nelly, I'll ne'er
    give you pain,
Down in the bower, just come for an hour,
  And the nipple shall be at your service
    again ! "

The Female Workwoman

An excellent new Smutty Song.

*Air—*REGENT STREET.

I am a lass that's young and free,
I've travelled the country round, d'ye see,
Because I'm a female of that kind,
That will have a workman to my mind.
All tradesmen I have had at will,
And tried their varions ways and skill,
And all that I have had, ere long
I'll quickly tell you in my song.

The carpenter he pleased me so,
At boarding he's the man, yeu know,
His hole he quickly guages out
With his gimblet long and stout.
His tools, indeed I do not jest,
Are always of the very best,
He wedges it with his taper pin,
Then with his mallet he drives it in.

The sawyer I found was the lad,
Who ever makes a female glad;
At my saw pit, without delay,
He worked with joy both night and day
If he worked above, I worked below,
And I had a machine, you know,
If his tools did ever get out of repair,
I sharpened them up, e'en to a hair.

The stone mason, he pleased me too,
For how to erect his pillar he knew,

He blocked my drain up, quite secure,
And placed two stones right bang before.
A tanner came, he was divine;
He tanned my leather very fine!
The reaper went to work straightway,
And very soon he mowed my hay.

A tinker next much time did spend,
He knew the way my kettle to mend;
He brought his heater to my sight,
And hammered my kettle with all his might.
The tinker was a hearty soul,
And when he had found out the hole,
To work with pleasure he did begin,
And quickly dropt his solder in.

A gardener pleased me well indeed,
He planted in my ground his seed;
And very soon my mould-pit, mute,
Convinced me it had taken root.
I liked his root, I must protest,
But he showed me a beet root I liked best;
But he found to plant it would not suit,
Cause my pot was too small for such large fruit.

A tailor came, a man quite fit,
And he found beneath my clothes a slit,
So he pulled his long needle out,
And stitched away so well and stout.
Of all the workmen I did see,
The tailor is the man for me,
Because he is a social soul,
And always ready to stop a hole.

71

Air—*Bill Bounce.*

In Fulham town, as people say,
A couple courted, night and day ;
So firm and constant were their loves,
They bill'd and coo'd like turtle doves.
So merrily pass'd their time away,
They did so often toy and play ;
The happiest couple that ever met,
Were Red-nose Jemmy and Bandy Bet.
 But in love affairs, when fortune frowns,
 There are so many ups and downs ;
 I don't know how true, but as I've been told,
 The hottest love is the soonest cold.

She servant was at a large cook-shop,
And Jemmy round the door would hop ;
And when his stomach began to gnaw,
She'd give him something to stop his maw.
Besides, she used to fill a bag,
As much as he could under wag ;
Then after all, his pockets to fill,
She'd go and rob her master's till.
 Oh dear, oh dear, to the devil she'll go,
 For serving her poor master so ,
 Upon my word, as I'm alive,
 Cheating play will never thrive.

And so it turn'd out, as you shall find,
With a fellow who cried out knives to grind ;
That stopt at her master's door with his barrow,
When Cupid pierced her with his arrow.
She brought him out a job to grind,
All the knives that she could find ;
And said, young man, I plainly see,
You are the one that shall grind for me.
 Her words did charm him, as she spoke,
 His wheel it flew round till it nearly broke ;
 With his barrow so clean, and his stones so
  wet,
 He kept grinding away for Bandy Bet.

Next day poor Jemmy found a check
Was put on his day's allowance of peck ;
For the grinder had been there with a large
  brown pan,
And carried off all the broken scan.
Day after day, week after week,
Poor Jemmy round the door did sneak :
She didn't care for him a jot,
For the grinder had done what he'd forgot.
 Oh dear, how could a woman do so,
 What a woman loves best he ought to know,
 For this said job, I do believe,
 Was first found out by Adam and Eve.

In six months time she lost her peace,
Because she got thick about the waist ;
The grinder from the town took flight,
As soon as he found that her skin got tight.
In nine months time, to crown her joy,
She brought in the world a thumping boy ;
And Jemmy to father it was the fool,
Although it was marked with the grinder's tool.
 The lads all said what are you at,
 You're never a going to be such a flat ;
 But I can't help it, 'cause, d'ye see,
 I 'spose as how it was to be.

When all was over, Jem paid for the job,
And the grinder again there shewed his nob ;
So when Jemmy goes out a walk to get,
The grinder goes grinding for Bandy Bet.
Again, I'm told. the job is done,
There's a daughter coming to play with the son ;
Now don't you think they're a d—d rum set,
The Grinder, and Jemmy, and Bandy Bet,
 But of Red-nose Jemmy pray don't make
  game,
 You or I may be served the same ;

A man can't tell. if he's ever such a don,
When his back is turned, what's going on.

I Will be a Mot

Now is it not a pity such a pretty girl as I Should be sent to a

Nun ne ry to pine a way and die But I won't be a Nun, No I

won't be a Nun, I'm so fond of pleasure that I cannot be a Nun.

I'm sure I can not tell, what the

mischief I have done, But my Mother of ten tells me that I must be a

Nun, But I wont be a Nun, No I wont be a Nun, I'm so fond of

pleasure that I cannot be a Nun.

A Slashing Rvmmy Parody on I won't be a Nun.

Now isn't it a pity,
  Such a cunning lass as I
Should ever die a virgin,
  Or for Roger have to sigh.
        I will be a mot,
        I shall be a mot,
          I'm so fond of Roger,
        That I will be a mot,

My mother often tells me
  How Roger she did dread,
And the shocking pain it cost her,
  When she lost her maidenhead ;
            But I will be, &c

I've got a little Fanny,
  That with hair is overspread,
And I'm sure it is a shame
  That its mouth should not be fed :
            So I will, &c.

I saw my cousin William, once,
  As naked as could be,
And he had a something 'twixt his thighs,
  That dangled to his knee !
            So I will, &c.

To sleep in bed all by myself,
  I'm sure it's very hard ;
I should like to have a stout young man,
  Who knows well how to mount guard.
            So I will, &c

I should like to have a youth, who me
  Would in his arms enfold,
Who would handle me and dandle me
  When my belly it was cold ;
            So I will be, &c.

I love that magic member
  That the men have 'neath their clothes,
I love squeezing I love Roger,
  And I love his ruby nose.
            So I will, &c

I like to lay upon my back,
  And use what I have got,
But my mother often tells me
  That I shan't be a mot.
            But I will, &c.

Young Robert rolled me in the grass,
  And gave me so much meat,
That, ever since, I'm really mad
  To have another treat.
            So I will, &c.

So, mother, don't be growling,
  For this I'd have you know,
I'll never die for want of meat,
  So a tailing I will go.
            And I w

A prime new smutty Song.

Air—" Derry down."

When Nature form'd man, as the story is told,
She created him in such a very small mould,
That when he was finish'd—tis true, I declare,
He'd a yard of good stuff stuck before him to
    spare.

For a short time this yard of good stuff, as I
    learn,
To but one purpose could man ever turn ;
'Twas a sort of ball cock, as the story you'll con,
Which the water did daily both turn off and on.

He was quite discontented with this, as I'm told,
For it often was frozen quite stiff with the cold ;
And he quickly found out—I'm indeed not in
    fun—
That to warm it it wanted much more than the
    sun !

So Nature created a woman the next,
And cast her in a mould that made her quite
    vext,
For she'd used all her stuff, ere her figure she'd
    done't,
Which left her a mighty great hole in the front !

When the woman beheld the man's yard of stuff,
You may guess that she was in a deuce of a
    huff ;
And she vowed by her honour, and likewise her
    soul,
That his yard was her right just to fill up her
    hole !

She teazed the poor man nearly out of his life,
So at length he complied just to banish the strife ;
He fill'd up her hole with his yard, I declare,
And he found that it fitted her just to a hair !

But he made a discovery strange—I'm no liar—
He found in her hole all his heart could desire;
When his yard it was stiff, and so cold too, what
    fun,
He found it could thaw it more quick than the
    sun !

From that time man, 'tis said, and its true, on
    my soul,
Was willing to fill up the poor woman's hole ;
Which she claims as her right, and with justice
    enough,
Whenever she pleases, man's yard of good stuff !

A PRIME NEW FLASH DITTY.

Tune — *Arthur O' Bradley.*

Come, listen awhile unto me,
You *Sheena's* of ev'ry degree;
I sing of a bit of a rout,
To which all the motts were asked out;
Togg'd in their best cloathes so grand,
At a bawdy-ken just by the Strand,
The baw'd had just come to some cash,
So determined she was to be flash;
She invited the blowens so free,
To dinner and also to tea;
She search'd all the streets for the *gals*,
And invited the whole of their pals;
And at night, what was better than all,
She gave all the blowens a ball!
    All rare blowens together,
    Were met at the bawdy-house ball!

And had you but witness'd the lot,
I'm sure you would ne'er have forgot,
There was leary, and bandy and lame
Goggle-eyed, humpy, and game,
There was Old Wriggle-stern Bet,
Black Len, with a face like jet;

Brazen-face Kitty and Peg,
Who had such a charming cork leg:
Blear-eyed Suke and her man,
Frisky Old Nelly and Fan;
Mother M'Casey so stout,
With her bubbies all dangling out,
Wry-mouth Jenny and Poll,
Sally, and bandy-legg'd Moll!
        All rare, &c.

The *Pensioners* came in a throng,
To mix with the blowens among,
There was costermongers and *pigs*,
Dustmen, coalheavers, and prigs,
There was thirty flash kiddies or more,
A couple to every w——e,
There was leary Bob Flummax so jolly,
Long-shanks and *Elephant's tolly*,
There was Billy the faker so sly,
Flash Joe who had only one eye,
The tall costermonger Ben Brown,
Who had kiss'd every girl on the town,
Some with their shirts hanging out,
Determined to make up the rout!
        All flash kiddies, &c.

The bawd got them plenty of scran,
Pigs chittlings fried in a pan;
Sheeps' jemmies to stuff in their croup,
Cow-heels, cocks'-head broth and pea soup,
Red herrings full fifty or more,
Baked taters and carrots galore,
Trotters to please the old cronies,
Faggots, and bread and polonies,
Gatter a deuce of a lot,
Gin in an old chamber pot;
The blowens were all quite gay,
They wolf'd ev'ry thing in their way,
They drank and they blow'd out their kite,
Oh! never was seen such delight! All, &c.

With the gatter they made very free,
Till the time it came round to have tea;
Ev'ry one drank twenty cups,
For they wouldn't take it by sups,
They proved they were none of them guffins,
They each put away thirty muffins;
Till at last the old bawd gave a squall,
" It's time to commence with the ball!"
The fiddler they stuck on a chair,
And to scrape he did quickly prepare;
Cried blear-eyed Sukey so arch,
" Come, play you old *bloat*, 'The Rogues
   March"
Said bandy-legged Moll, " that's no use,
" You old buffer play 'Petticoats loose!"
                           For, we're all, &c.

They took all the chairs from the room,
The bawd she beat time with the broom,
They all did so merrily prance,
They jig, ree·, caper and dance,
The *gals* just to give themselves ease,
Pull'd their petticoats up to their knees;
Kitty, the stupid young w——e,
Fell smack on her rump on the floor,
She scream'd out with horror and dread,
For her cloathes flew all over her head,
And the kiddies all feasted their eyes,
On a something not far from her thighs,
And they all declared I am sure,
They'd ne'er seen a better before! So, &c.

They danced while they sometimes did boose,
Till they all felt inclined for a snoose,
Then every one of the gals,
Selected two coves for their pals,
And for fear it should not be enough,
They strip't themselves all into buff,
And having display'd all their charms,
They rush'd into each other's arms,
Of crowding not being in dread,
They laid full six in a bed;
They huddled and cuddled together,
Because they were birds of a feather,
They kiss'd one another so true,
And did—what we all like to do!
         So they all got happy together
         That met at the Bawdy-house ball!

"THE MAY-POLE."

("COME LASSES AND LADS.")

Willy has got his Jill..... And Jocky has got his Joan,... To
ev'_ry lad did take,.... His hat off to his lass, And

Chorus.

jig it, jig it, jig it, jig it, jig it up and down. Sing tol de rol de
ev'_ry maid did curt_sey, curt_sey, curt sey on the grass.

rol de rol, Sing tol de rol lol li da;... Sing tol de rol de lol de rol lol, oh!

tol de rol lol di da....

A prime new bawdy Song.

Air—" *The Maypole.*"

In the summer time,
    Oh, isn't it prime,
In a grove hid from the eye,
    To lay a lass,
    On the verdant grass,
And tickle her on the sty?
    To lift the modest veil,
        Which hides her secret charms;
    To tickle her bubbies, her belly, her tail,
        And roll her in your arms!

    The belly so fair,
    And bedeck'd with hair,
And the sweet little crevice so red;
    The buttock so plump,
    The thigh—the rump,
Where luxury round is spread!
    When belly to belly is met,
        And limbs round limbs entwine;
    With a wriggle, and jiggle, and sighing, and
        dying—
        Oh, God! is it not divine.

    Such rural sport
    I always court;
Quite young I the sport did learn;
    I got Sally Box
    Among the haycocks,
And gave her *a cock* in return!
    A lecherous creature was she,
        With a cuckoo's nest mossy and ruff;
    She huddled me, cuddled ime, handled me,
        findled me,
        But I never could give her enough!

    Then Susan, the jade,
    The fresh dairy-maid,
I met her a milking the cow,
    With the udder in hand,
    Quite entranced I did stand,
And I felt sure I cannot tell how!
    She twisted the udder about,
        And shew'd me her seat of bliss;
    Saying—" Roger, I know you an udder can't
        shew
        That will suit such a dairy as this!"

    In a moment or two,
    I the gem brought to view,
Mighty love! how she open'd her eyes—
    Admired its strength—
    Its beauty—its length—
Its vigour—its boldness—its size?
    But, in spite of its being so big,
        She seized it with lustful delight,
    And in less than a minute she found out a wig
        Which hid it completely from sight.

    So thus with the fair
    I such extacy share—
I am known by the country around;
    Each damsel, with joy,
    Will my rudder employ,
For a better can no where be found,
    The sweet mossy cave is my pride,
        Oh, what yields such exquisite bliss;
    And as long as I wag, I never will lag,
        But roll in such pleasure as this.

A regular Funny Original Song, now first
  printed.—Air—*Betsy Baker*.

In London-town, as stories tell,
  (To mention it's my duty)
A lady once in style did dwell,
  Fam'd for her wit and beauty.
She had a spouse—a loving spouse—
  Who never strove to teaze her;
But when they went to bed, indeed,
  He did every thing to please her.
                  With his tooral, &c.

This lady had a footman smart,
  And nothing but a good-un;
But yet he in complexion was
  Black as a large black pudding!
But when for brandy he was sent,
  I'm sure you'd scarcely think it,
Young Smutto had such a liquorish tooth,
  That best part he would drink it.
                  With his tooral, &c.

His mistress soon suspected him,
  And vow'd to give him no quarter,
For after he had drank his whack,
  He filled it up with water;
So she at last determined was
  To stop his pilfering humour,
And vow'd her brandy, he again,
  Should ne'er be a consumer.
                  With his tooral, &c.

One day he took a little sup,
  While she at lunch was seated—
The lady twigg'd him on the sly,
  And thus her mind repeated :—
You rogue, you've at the brandy been,
  You'll put me in a foment,
You've guzzled down full half-a-pint—
  I saw you just this moment.
                  With your tooral, &c.

Oh Misses !—how can you say so,
  Cried Smutto in a crack then,
You neber could see me, I'm sure,
  Vhile me behind you back then.
You simple rogue, the lady said,
  I very well could mind ye,
Because as well as in my head,
  Why I've got eyes behind me.
              With my tooral, &c.

Oh dear, cried Smutto to himself,
  Dese be queer days, od rottem,
For missee hab eyes in her head,
  And eyes too in her bottom!
But if dat be de got tam truth,
  It bothers my nob quite no,
Me cannot see dese backside eyes,
  So dey must be out o' sight now.
              With her tooral, &c.

It happen'd one day after this,
  She on the sofa was sleeping,
And master Smutto happen'd to,
  That way to be a-creeping

Oh, oh, said he, dis be good chance,
  Dat sleeping so me find her,
So me vill take vou peep, to see
  If she hab eyes behind her.
              With her tooral, &c.

So quickly he removed the clothes,
  Her beauteous charms displaying—
Around, about her, ev'ry where,
  Quite pleased, he was surveying.
At last a something he did spy,
  So took a loving peep, sir ;
Said he—oh, misse got von eye,
  But dat be fast asleep, sir.
              Tooral, &c.
While he was feasting thus his eyes,
  In bounced his angry master,
And gazed, with fury and surprise,
  At this, so strange disaster.
No touchee, master," Smutto cried,
  My missee I sleepee find her,
And so me thought me peep to see
  If she had eyes behind her.
              Ri tooral, &c.

The W-hole of the Ladies

Words and Music by RICHARD LEVERIDGE (1670–1758).

1. When migh - ty roast beef was the Eng - lish - man's food, It en
2. But since we have learnt from ef - fem - in - ate France, To
3. Our fa - thers of old were ro - bust, stout, and strong, And

1. no - bled our hearts, and en rich - ed our blood, Our sol - diers were brave and our
2. eat of their *rag - outs*, as well as to dance, We're fed up with no - thing but
3. kept o - pen house with good cheer all day long, Which made their plump ten - ants re

1. cour - tiers were good, Oh! the roast beef of old Eng - land! And oh! for old Eng - land's roast
2. vain *com - plais - ance*, Oh! the roast beef of old Eng - land! And oh! for old Eng - land's roast
3. joice in the song, Oh! the roast beef of old Eng - land! And oh! for old Eng - land's roast

1. beef. . . . .
2. beef. . . . .
3. beef. . . . .

90

A out-and-out Amatory Song, now first printed.

Air.—*Oh, the roast beef of old England.*

Of all the sweet pleasure that mortal man
    knows,
There's none like the pleasure enjoyment be-
    stows,
Which dwells in the ladies sweet little moss
    rose,
  So give me the w-*hole* of the ladies!
  The w-hole of the ladies for me!

The little brunette with the roguish black eye,
The sweet little nymph with the delicate thigh,
And the sweet little grove that grows very nigh,
  Give charms to the w-*hole* of the ladies,
  Oh, the w-*hole* of the ladies for me!

The lad of sixteen, feels uneasy 'tis plain,
He's hot as a fire—seeks ease all in vain,
But he very soon finds a relief to his pain,
When he meets with the w-*hole* of the ladies,
  Oh, the w-hole of the ladies for me!

The parson so pious may preach 'till all blue,
'Bout the spirit and flesh; but you'll find **this is**
    true,
When he walks from the pulpit—where he **wan-**
    ders too,
  Is the sweet little w-*hole* of the ladies,
  Oh the w-hole of the ladies for me!

On a cold winter's night, when the frost nips our
    nose,
If we're stiff, there s a thing, which can thaw us
    all knows,
Meet a beautiful girl, and get under the clothes,
  Then how sweet is the w-*hole* of the ladies,
  Oh, the w-hole of the ladies for me!

Its's the seat of such extacy, spot of delight,
Our comfort, our transport, by day and by night,
Then bless it, caress it, when it meets our
    sight,
  We all came from the w-*hole* of the ladies!
  So the w-hole of the ladies for me!

———

ToAst.—Adam's *root* which Eve planted in
    her little garden and which we all sprung
    from.

The Bride

The Sea! the Sea! the o - pen Sea! The blue, the fresh, the

e - ver free the e - ver e - ver free!

Without a mark, without a bound, It runneth the earth's wide regions

round; It plays with the clouds, it mocks the skies, Or

like a cradled creature lies, Or like a cradled crea- -ture lies.

Storm . . . . . should come, . . . and a- -wake . . . . . the deep, What

crescendo for

matter? what matter? I shall ride and sleep. What matter? what

matter? I shall ride and sleep.

Boatswain's Whistle.

A Famous Amatory Parody on " *The Sea !*"
sung at the Cider Cellars.

My bride! my bride! my luscious frisky
    bride,
No other one I'll kiss beside !
With belly plump—and round and fair,
And your little spot all clad with hair !
You make me queer—when I feast my eyes,
On your private charms—and your ivory
    thighs !
I'm on my bride !—I'm on my bride ?
Till from her floods the lecherous tide,
And her eyes with lust and passion glow,
For the treat I'm giving her down below !
If her belly should swell—which oft I fill,
What matter ! what matter ! my bride I will
    ride still';

I love, oh, how I love to ride,
My hot, my wheedling, coaxing bride,
While every throb, and every heave,
Does near of senses her bereave,
And she takes the *staff of life* in hand,
'Till she makes each pulse and fibre stand !
I love her C——!—I love her C——!
And on it I will ever be,
In spite of every randy whore,
I'll kiss my luscious bride the more !
And when the devil shall for me glide,
He shall find *me lock'd* in the arms of my randy
    bride !